Call Me ill

T. S. Banks

ISBN # 978-1-522-08834-9

Call Me ill/ T. S. Banks

Table of Contents

Part 1: When I Knew It was Time to go to the Hospital

Untitled	7
Sometimes When I feel Sick	8
Epidemic of Confinement	9
Avoidance	11
Grief	12
Plight	13
Symphony	15

Part 2: Waiting Room

Waiting Room	17

Part 3: The Emergency Room

Room 11	20
You're Just So Sensitive	22

Part 4: B6/5 UW Hospital Psyche Ward

Inverted Conversations   26
The Diagnosis   25

Part 5: When I Came Home

How Does It Fell   29
August   28
Time Heals All Wounds   30
Ode To My Scars: Home   31

Dedication

To My QTIB's
Queer, Trans, & Intersex Black Folx

PART 1: When I knew, it was time to go to the Hospital

Sometimes it feels like everything is falling apart
My limbs and joints departing from themselves clothed in
black skin. The gape between joint and bone
Loose saggy skin searching foreground
Skin to skin contact
My hands and feet and elbow and stomach, all left with a
tingling sensation
My heart flutters and pounds walking every step
Not sure i found home yet

Sometimes when I feel sick –

I disappear into another world

2. Lose my grip
3. Binge
4. insulin shots, 6 times a day
5. morbid obesity,
6. The schizophrenia
7. mania –
8. the depression,
9. the sex,
        that I wish would last longer
        than the second
        person to tell me
                I was

        beautiful and meant it

When I feel myself

10. fly the cusp of what is real
        always a contrast

        two spirits
        health and sickness,

11. juxtaposed

        Beside myself inside my head,
            everything feels
        intense
            I can't name it

12.   The babble.
        Them noises,
        pinned my ear to the wall
leave me rigid.
        a closed mouth
        a tear
        a smile

Epidemic of the confinement

My restitution is no longer taken as tender
The world feels I am too depreciated to exploit
existing Black is no longer enough
Are we enough to hold each other's secrets?

Enough –
A word I'm not strong enough to contemplate

Delayed
            when they tell me psychosis –
Is just a different way of thinking – a pause on the
ability to understand feeling

Lately I been feeling absent
Blew all the money
Knew I might not see the rest of the Son
When morning looks bleak
I look to become more
Less mess I'm in right now

Is it a sin to plan the end?
The end is more than a wish for relief

How I tried to erase my skin with a silver blade
the sudden drop in my voice

I moan
For peace
Comfort
To peace the underbelly of my uterus
Holding a secret,
Panicking and Night sweats
I have nothing else to give,
But apologize for myself

My face reads all the emotion

       Contradicted and I say "I'm fine"
But you see this streaming tear –

I have nothing left to give

Avoidance

In Order to avoid the hospital
I stay pent up and ill in my home
Trying to up the dose on my own and silently
Go unnoticed

I can't place my name.
Out of place inside my home
Paying to be a part of something I don't own.

Grief

thursday, and in shock,
i try to keep quiet.
i hear all these sounds.
i hear all these sounds.
her breath forced through a machine,
tears of a son hitting the tile by her bed,

grief is a toothless smile
tearing the tissue of my heart.
i stare into the corner,
head sunken into pillow,
tears murmuring a hushed prayer
haunted by the last memory-
a machine and mist pumping air into her brittle lungs.

grief sits aloft my room,
reads through my books,
escapes my throat, and delivers a yelp.
everyone can hear.
everyone can see.
grief is excepted, depression not tolerated

i wish we had more time.

Plight

depression is water
laced in the hairs of –
my dermis
smooth in the palm,
brittle and salty,

my palm cradles a cure,
prescribed by doctors who
already gave up on my recovery.

give me anything to silence
discomfort.
any outcome they earn a dollar.
i stay wet with grief,

depression is cloth
like cuffs around my wrist –
the color behind my lids
when they label me psychotic,
and restraint is a cure,
when I pray to God for a
savior
or a pill to return me back home
stable and *normal*,
able to be loved

i question God's love for me.
how he made me sad
and unimportant.
            depression is unimportant,

physicians that violate every
thought i once held secret.
try to name me ill, and incompetent,
anything but a child of God,

depression is guilt for
missed birthdays and graduations,
money wasted on tickets,
the concerts awaiting my applause.

tears that my mother is tired of wiping,
9 scars that haunt my forearm

I'm tired of crying
saying curses to every morning I awaken
looking at shrinking pill bottles and
wondering when I can exist without them.

depression is a weapon
and I have been assaulted

Symphony

Sometimes my mind cries
And the only way to silence
the whimpers of breath lost in flooding waters is to crawl
into stillness,
Melt into the awkward stiffness
Cough a stuttered mute staccato can be interpreted as
words
Cold read me as sheet music
Watch my face contort and body quake as I try to
arrange melancholy on the staffed lines
For each emotion, they watch
        Applaud when the symphony is finished
I retreat back to compose another
This time I am andante, and beautifully scattered over
voice overs
In fractions, cut
        portioned for their orchestra
Caught in the string of their conductor

PART 2: Waiting Room

Waiting room

We arrive on the outside
My legs stiff
      screaming to turn the car around
The sliding door opens

There is a plastic bouquet of flowers
A question
A answer
I look down
Ashamed she can't see where it hurts
The radio calls me a psyche patient

She speaks three syllables
I answer and walk
I am not caged yet

Magenta cuff around my forearm
Pressure and pulse
Light in my eyes
Light in my ears
Light above me

Are you suicidal
Yes.
Are you in danger
Yes
Do you hear voices
Yes.
Have you tried to self-harm
No.
I'm having a hard time.

Shake and nod
Yes. No.
I shrug

One wheelchair
child whispers questions
Child points at me
Child whispers question

Child stares at me.

The ceiling changes colors
I try to touch the ceiling
Touch my lap
Folded against a chair.

A nurse utters three syllables
My chair is moving

Part 3: The Emergency Room

Room 11

hear the ticking of florescent light
on the floor
in the corner

room 11

scream

enfold your words into your belly,
fetal and still
push needle into thigh or whatever
flesh is open,
close,
drift home.

room 11

take 3 pills, three. times. daily.

caused me mute and available,
caught in the transfer,
broke. my words. Into.
repeated syllables
they broke.
me into syl.la.bles
heard, not seen

return to room 11

undusted corner
stripped.
teddy bear
scream.
Injections.
9 scars –
left forearm.

Room 11

You're Just so Sensitive

Echoed in the hallway of the doctor's office
my doctor is always cold and white,

i feel everything so deeply
why my father always leaves me
in the mental ward,
no word just a hug and a conversation
          with my mother in the car ride home

it hurts him to know
his son isn't tough like him
dress tough, but can't stop crying
he commands my tears to stop
you're just so sensitive

my mind broke yesterday,
they waited a whole night
to fill my mouth with medicine
the doctors have said

if i regain speech
                    i'm a miracle

Part 4: B6/5 UW Hospital

B-Six/Five
When I know I have to be locked away
because I am unstable
When I'm begging for another pill
Or something to make me know these
feelings are normal

Inverted conversations

I feel like an inanimate object
Confined to predetermined space and meaning
        there is no growth for an object less than human

others capitalize on this moment.
A shell, my ears are clay,
        Mold me into anything.

The Diagnosis

Female
23
12/30/1987
Black
Diagnosis: Personality Disorder Unspecified
Dictation:
23 Year Old Black Female. Being Sent Home Today. Will ReCover. If She Covers Up Parts of HerSelf. Confused about her Sexuality and Religion.

Dr. Freedom:
"I'm not saying that being gay is wrong but you think it is. That's why you hear voices. It's just your inner thoughts and conscious coming to the surface. We're taking you off the Haldol and starting you back on your anti-depressants. Really only therapy will cure you of this, because we can not help you here.
We don't cure issues of morality."

Part 5: When I Came Home

How Does it Feel

Like I got 1 head and 8 arms
Some above my head
Others around my waste
Some just floating

When I have sight of my chest
And my hair and my clothes, that still don't tell the story
I lose it

How does it feel,

Repressed anger
Sitting at the edge of my esophagus
A burp like skipping hopscotch, do I reach rage,
ingest this seed,
breathe off the cliff

How does it feel

Looking at the side of my face, counting the hairs on my
chin, feeling the restraint under my chin, hearing my
voice, seeing my hands, grabbing any words to greet the
morning

To face the door opening to the hall
To the car
To open the car door
To step inside any place

Or know that today should be different
A diagnosis looming over the choices
When I want to change all the choices given to me

To check two binary boxes and remember that every
change that I need
Cost too many sacrifices,
It feels like too much to hold on to

It feels like too much to choke down in the car and
pretend the cold winter air brought your hands with
Kleenex crumpled from your coat

Feels like too much to say that it's hard not having the
choices
To have only two options
that don't feel comfortable
Like itchy skin, a sweater, a rash that belongs to you
A president that ain't yours
The unsafe choice

An intersection of black and love, and true
Of black and queer and trans and masculine and parallel
lines that blend together
to tell me that being black and disabled is already too
heavy, too much time, too much sensitive, add an
oppression,

not worth the representation and access
It feels like slavery been on me
And new links on my chain, new hands on the whip
Feels like they gonna keep killing me too
Feels like they gonna keep killing me too

Feels like too much
Feels like too much
For freedom to be issued to me
Feels like too much I gotta pay to be free,
Feels like too much to fight for
Feels like it's to heavy
Feel like I'm too heavy

August.
Trans* People Murdered in 2017

Mesha Caldwell
Jamie Lee Wounded Arrow
JoJo Striker
Jaquarrius Holland
Keke Collier
Chyna Gibson
Ciara McElveen
Alphonza Watson
Chay Reed
Kenneth Bostick
Sherrell Faulkner
Kenne McFadden
Kendra Marie Adams
Ava Le'Ray Barrin
Ebony Morgan
TeeTee Dangerfield
Gwynevere River Song
Kiwi Herring

Time Heals All Wounds

Time crawling
I hold my head in palms cleaning the dust of barren
hands between the slits of my fingers

Chest wall agape, the beat of my heart mimicking the
staggered steps I took home after the chastising of my
masculinity

A breasted body doesn't get compassion in the transition
of their boyhood

In the wait of hormones
tissue that never healed

Hide in shame-lit cloth
Burn in front of mirror

wounded on the alter

God is still silent

Ode to My Scars: Home

Raised like fist, lay tan scars
Juxtaposed between rebellion and home

Reminiscence over the red trickled on my car floor

Now scars are celebration
Proof I did work to find the apostrophe in my name
Why my smile is so big

Catastrophe in the rebirth of me
Only ravaged to be rebuilt

I find solace in the rubble
To know something wrecked, can stand again

But this foundation of dermis will always have a
cornerstone –
set neatly on left forearm

remind me, I made it

Made in the USA
Lexington, KY
12 September 2017